ANCIENT AFRICA
AND THE
ATLANTIC
SLAVE TRADE

◧◧

MODERN CURRICULUM PRESS

◎ Program Consultants

SHARON HARLEY, PH.D.
Associate Professor/Acting Director
African American Studies
University of Maryland

STEPHEN MIDDLETON, PH.D.
Assistant Professor of History
North Carolina University

◎ Program Reviewers

JACOB H. CARRUTHERS, PH.D.
Professor/Associate Director
Center For Inner City Studies
Northeastern Illinois University

BARBARA EMELLE, PH.D.
Associate Director of
Curriculum and Instruction
New Orleans Public Schools

PAUL HILL, JR.
Executive Director,
East End Neighborhood House
Cleveland, Ohio

SUBIRA KIFANO
Teacher Advisor
Language Development Program
for African American Studies
Los Angeles Public Schools

MARY SHEPHERD LESTER
Director of Mathematics
Dallas Public Schools

LINDA LUPTON
Curriculum Coordinator
Cleveland Public Schools

GWENDOLYN MORRIS
Instructional Support Teacher
Philadelphia Public Schools

THOMASINA PORTIS
Director, Multicultural/Values Education
Washington, D.C. Public Schools

DOROTHY W. RILEY
Librarian and Author
Detroit, Michigan

Illustrators

Lou Pappas, Chapter Bottom Borders; Beatrice Brooks, 8 *(bottom)*, 14-15; Cheryl Hanna, 22; Jennifer Hewitson, 31; Barbara Higgins Bond, 17, 34; Holly Jones, 7, 30, 36; Dorothy Novick, 20, 37; Jan Palmer, 25 *(top & bottom)*, 38, 39.

Photo Credits

18 *(top)*, 24 *(bottom)*, 27 *(bottom)*, Abbas/Magnum; 38-39, The Bettmann Archive; 11 *(bottom)*, Dianne Blell/Peter Arnold, Inc.; 12 *(bottom)*, Bruce Coleman Inc.; 9 *(middle)*, Comstock, Inc.; 21, M. Courtney-Clarke; 39, 42, Culver Pictures, Inc.; 19 *(bottom)*, V. Englebert/Leo de Wys Inc.; 10 *(middle-bottom)*, 11 *(top)*, P.A. Ferrazzini, Musee Barber-Mueller; 9 *(bottom)*, Tomas D.W. Friedmann/Photo Researchers, Inc.; 29 *(top)*, Galerie Kamer, Collection of Mr. & Mrs. Allen Gerdau; 18 *(bottom)*, 19 *(top)*, 26 *(top)*, 27 *(top)*, 32-33, 40 *(top)*, 40 *(middle)*, The Granger Collection; 9 *(top)*, George Holton/Photo Researchers, Inc.; 26 *(bottom)*, 28, Wolfgang Kaehler; 29 *(bottom)*, The Mansell Collection; 35, The United Nations; 10 *(top)*, Martin Vanderwall/Leode Wys, Inc.; 4-5, Luis Villota/The Stock Market; 12 *(top)*, Douglas Waugh/Peter Arnold, Inc.; 41, Schomburg Center for Reasearch in Black Culture/The New York Public Library/Astor, Lenox and Tilden Foundations; 24 (top), Trustees of the British Museum; 16, Beryl Goldberg.

Map Credits

Ortelius Design, 4, 6, 8, 14, 22, 32.

Acknowledgments

Every reasonable effort has been made to locate the ownership of copyrighted material and to make due acknowledgment. Any errors or omissions will be gladly rectified in future editions. p. 27: Excerpt from BEFORE THE MAYFLOWER A HISTORY OF BLACK AMERICA by Lerone Bennett Jr. Published by Johnson Publishing Company. © 1961, 1962, 1964, 1969, 1982. p. 28: Excerpt from AFRICA THE DAYS OF EXPLORATION edited by Roland Oliver and Caroline Oliver. Published by Prtentice Hall, Inc. p. 34, 39, 40: Excerpts from THE CLASSIC SLAVE NARRATIVES edited by Henry Louis Gates, Jr. Published by Penguin USA.

Design & Production: TWINC, Catherine Wahl, Kurt Kaptur
Executive Editor: Marty Nordquist
Project Editor: June M. Howland

MODERN CURRICULUM PRESS
13900 Prospect Road, Cleveland, Ohio 44136
Simon & Schuster • A Paramount Communications Company

Based on *The African American Experience: A History* published by Globe Book Company © 1992.

ISBN 0-8136-4955-2 (Reinforced Binding)   ISBN 0-8136-4956-0 (Paperback)

10 9 8 7 6 5 4 3 2 1   98 97 96 95 94

CONTENTS

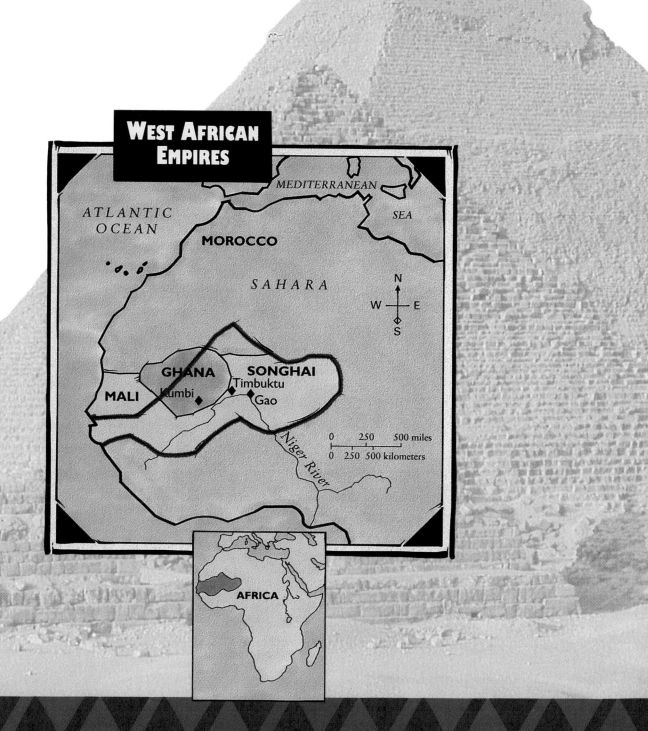

WEST AFRICAN EMPIRES

MEDITERRANEAN

SEA

ATLANTIC
OCEAN

MOROCCO

SAHARA

N
W   E
S

GHANA   SONGHAI
Kumbi   Timbuktu
MALI   Gao

Niger River

0   250   500 miles
0   250 500 kilometers

AFRICA

HISTORY
SPEAKS

Africa is the second largest continent in the world. It is not known for sure what ancient people called this land. The name Africa may have come from the Greek word *aphrike*, which means "without cold," or from the Latin word *aprica* which means "sunny."

In the oldest of times, the continent of Africa is where people first lived. Spear points, fishhooks, and parts of human skeletons are a few of the things that have been found there. If you are an African American, your ancestors came from this great continent.

Egypt (EE-jipt) is one of the oldest countries that we have information about today. The Nile River in Egypt was the water of life for the ancient people of East Africa. Early Egyptians farmed, traded, and lived along this great river. The Nile River formed important links between the peoples of Africa and people in other parts of the ancient world.

While Egypt was developing, other areas of Africa were also building civilizations. South of Egypt the kingdoms of Kush and Axum were growing. Buildings and sculptures from this time show that Egyptians not only shared ideas with these kingdoms but borrowed ideas from them as well.

Sharing ideas encouraged people from Egypt and other East African kingdoms to move south and west across the continent. From their settlements grew three great West African kingdoms. These kingdoms were Ghana (GAH-nah), Mali (MAH-lee), and Songhai (son-GAY). ▲

1

The history of ancient Africa is filled with rich stories of its lands and peoples. The earliest great kingdom of West Africa was Ghana (GAH-nah). It was wealthy, powerful, and well-respected by surrounding kingdoms. Ghana's power came from the trading of gold, salt, and other items with its neighbors. During its strongest years, Ghana was ruled by some very wise kings. ◗◗

THE EMPIRE OF GHANA

ATLANTIC OCEAN

SAHARA

N
W · E
S

GHANA
Kumbi ◆

Niger River

0   250   500 miles
0 250 500 kilometers

King Tunka Manin seated on his throne in ancient Ghana.

THE EMPIRE OF GHANA

The drums beat loudly as King Tunka Manin (TUN-kah MAN-in) of Ghana entered his palace court. Dressed in silk and covered with jewels he took his seat on a *throne* made of gleaming gold. Before him sat the lesser kings and chiefs of his huge *empire*. This night in the year 1065, he would listen to the problems of his people.

Behind the king's throne stood the finest warriors from among his 200,000 soldiers. They held shields of iron and gold-handled swords. Outside pranced his horses wearing gold harnesses. Pedigreed dogs with collars of gold and silver barked at arriving camel drivers. Such great splendor was just a small part of the wealth of the ancient African empire of Ghana.

So rich was his kingdom, that Tunka Manin was called lord of the gold. So powerful were his warriors that he was also called warrior king or Ghana. His kingdom then came to be known as Ghana.

Ghana was an advanced civilization located on rolling *grasslands* between the jungles of the Congo and the dry Sahara. The boundaries of the kingdom were not fixed because they changed with the fortunes of King Tunka Manin. The people built cities, farmed the land, raised their families, and lived peacefully with their neighbors.

The Silent Trade

Tunka Manin's mighty army and wealth were partly responsible for Ghana's greatness. The riches earned by the trade routes he controlled contributed also.

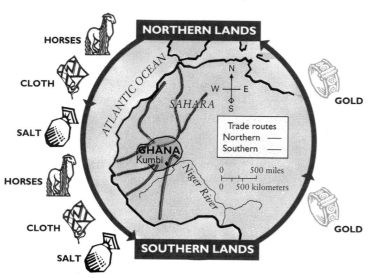

Trade in ancient Ghana.

Tunka Manin was a wise man. He recognized that his kingdom needed salt, and his lands were poor in this *mineral.* To the people of West Africa, the value of salt was almost equal to the value of gold. It was not only used to preserve food. It had to be eaten regularly to help keep moisture in the body.

Tunka Manin knew of a way to obtain salt and build up his own supplies of gold. Ghana lay between huge salt mines in the north and valuable gold mines in the south. So he allowed trade on his lands between people of the south and people of the north.

Caravans of camels were a common sight in ancient Ghana. Traders from the north would sigh in relief as they reached Kumbi (KOOM-bee), its capital city. They traveled over the *desert* for nearly

Africans set out their goods as part of the silent trade.

Top: Salt waiting to be transported by camel caravan.
Right: Before salt can be transported it is cut into bars.

six months to reach Kumbi. They carried huge loads of goods to trade.

When the caravans arrived, the northern traders beat a drum to alert the **merchants** of their approach. The **silent trade** would begin. This silent trade was necessary because there was no common language spoken between many of the different peoples of Africa. Most trading was done quickly and silently.

The northern traders laid their salt, fine cloths, wheat, and dried fruits on the ground. Then they moved out of sight to wait. The merchants of the south came forward and looked over the goods. Leaving their payment of gold, they stepped away also. Then the traders approached again and accepted the payment. Nodding to each other, they beat the drum to signal that the trade was complete. All of this happened without a single word being spoken.

CULTURE CORNER

MUSIC! MUSIC! MUSIC!

Harps and horns, drums and flutes, xylophones and zithers... These are musical instruments that were played by people in ancient Africa and have become a part of music today. The people of ancient times made music a part of their religious ceremonies and celebrations. Music was a part of daily life. What do you think these instruments were first made of? If you said wood, metal, animal skins, bones, and horns you were right.

The instruments that you see here have always been important in the culture of Ghana, and other African nations. In fact, they are important in American culture too. If you like modern jazz, blues, or rock-and-roll, you are enjoying music that had its roots in ancient Africa. How does music play a part in your life today?

The Capital City of Kumbi

Kumbi became a rich and colorful market center. Merchants from all over northern and western Africa came there to *barter* or trade goods. King Tunka Manin made money on every trade. He set up his own *tax* laws. Every buyer or seller paid a tax to him on the goods they traded. Tunka Manin's kingdom grew very wealthy.

Products other than salt or gold were also traded in the crowded markets of Kumbi. People who had been captured in wars and *enslaved* by their captors were sold to passing caravans. This did not trouble the people of Kumbi, or other people of Africa, since the buying and selling of people had taken place throughout the world since the beginning of time.

Most *captives* became servants or farm laborers. Many were not enslaved forever and could earn or buy their freedom. Others were freed by becoming members of the families to whom they were enslaved.

Top: Muslim mosque made with dried sand, mud and wood.
Bottom: Gold traded by Africans was often carved into beautiful designs.

As was common at that time, ancient Kumbi was a city divided. Kumbi was not divided because of war, but because the people had different religious beliefs. The people of Ghana worshipped many gods while the people to the north worshipped Allah. The people of the north were Arab **Muslims** who believed in *Islam*—a religion based on the teachings of Muhammad (moo-HAM-uhd).

King Tunka Manin often traded with the Muslims although he was faithful to his own religion. He believed in religious freedom and allowed his people to practice the religion of Islam if they chose. Muslims lived in the half of the city named Kumbi. The other half, called Al Ghaba (al-GAH-bah), was the home of the king.

No two parts of a city could be more different. Kumbi had twelve *mosques* (MOSKS), which are Muslim places of worship. The homes of many advisors and teachers were also located there. Among these buildings were large vegetable gardens, many wells of drinking water, and a large marketplace.

THE RICHNESS OF AFRICA

The year is 1070. Your caravan is bringing salt, cloth, dried fruit, and horses to trade in Ghana. What will you be trading for? Probably gold, ivory, and diamonds.

Would you trade for the same goods today? The wealth of Africa has not changed since ancient times. It is the largest producer of gold and diamonds in the world. Africa also produces huge amounts of petroleum, cobalt, platinum, copper, and uranium.

The richness of Africa does not end there. It supplies cocoa beans, cashews, cassava, cloves, vanilla beans, and timber from its great forests. Bananas, coffee, peanuts, rubber, and sugar are more of Africa's products.

What about the ivory trade? Africans have realized that the killing of elephants to obtain ivory must stop. There are many wildlife preserves across the continent where the elephants and other animals are protected by laws.

So, if you have traveled in a car, or eaten a banana lately, your life has been touched by the great continent of Africa.

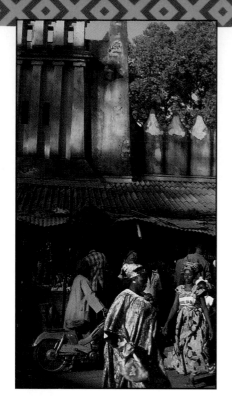

Kumasi is modern Ghana's second largest city. People there wear bold traditional and western clothes.

The city of Al Ghaba was more like a walled park. Inside its walls were the king's palace, his court, and the houses of many of his subjects. Outside the wall was a forest. There the king's scholars and religious counselors lived. The forest was a sacred place, and few people were allowed to enter it.

Tunka Manin's strong relations with the Muslims helped add to the empire's many years of peace. It also brought him wealth through increased trade with the Muslim people of the north. At its peak, ancient Ghana had a population of several million people and a territory of about 250,000 square miles.

By the 1100s, however, Ghana began to decline in power. A series of droughts had hurt the farmers and their crops. There were fewer goods to trade, so less gold came into the kingdom. The armies had fewer warriors. Ghana became open to attacks from Muslim invaders from the northwest. The mission of these invaders was to *conquer* new lands to spread the religion of Islam. After thirty years of fighting, Ghana was weakened. The Muslim invaders won the kingdom, but Ghana was quickly falling to ruins. ▨

GHANA TODAY

Location: Ghana is in West Africa, south of the location of the ancient kingdom

Capital: Accra

Size: 92,100 square miles, about the size of Missouri

Population: 13,892,000

Major groups: Aka, Ewe, Ga, Moshi-Dagomab peoples

TALK ABOUT IT

◎ How did the geography and the location of Ghana affect everyday life? How does the geography and location of where you live affect things that you do?

◎ Salt made the difference between life and death to the people of Ghana. What in your daily life has that same value to you? Name at least five items, in order of importance, that you could not live without.

◎ How did Tunka Manin treat people of different religions and backgrounds that came to live in his capital? How is this the same as or different than how various groups are treated in your school? In your city?

WRITE ABOUT IT

You have read about caravan travelers who used silent trading. But what if they could have spoken to each other? What would they have said? Create a conversation between the caravan traders from the north and the southern merchants from the beginning of the trade until the end. Try writing your own dialogue for a silent trade.

2

~~~~~~~~~~

By 1235, the area of West Africa which included Ghana was ruled by fierce Muslims. These Muslims would be the rulers of the next great African kingdom—Mali (MAH-lee). They were the first of a long line of Muslim leaders who controlled much of West Africa in ancient times. ◆◆

Sundiata faces Sumanguru for the first time.

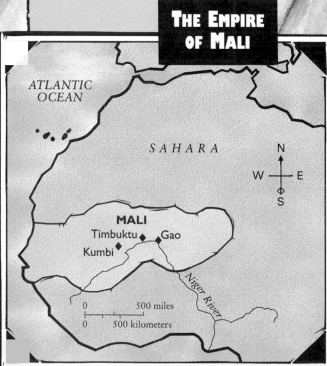

THE EMPIRE OF MALI

ATLANTIC OCEAN

SAHARA

N
W · E
S

MALI
Timbuktu ◆ ◆ Gao
Kumbi ◆

Niger River

0   500 miles
0   500 kilometers

THE EMPIRE OF MALI

The African kingdom of Mali gradually rose to greatness out of the ruins of Ghana. One of Mali's earliest leaders was a Muslim named Sundiata (SOON-dee-AH-tah).

The story of how Sundiata came to power is a well-known legend in West Africa. It tells of how Sundiata overcame an attack by a ruthless king, to grow up to be a king himself—the King of Mali. It is told this way:

A cruel king, Sumanguru (SOO-man-GOO-roo), killed eleven of twelve sons of the ruling Muslim family. The twelfth son, Sundiata, was born very sick and was so weak he could not even stand. Feeling sorry for the boy and believing he would soon die, Sumanguru spared his life. Then Sumanguru took over the family's kingdom.

Though Sundiata's body was weak, his will was strong. Gradually, and in great pain, he forced himself to move, then to stand, and then to walk. As he grew stronger, he learned to ride horses and fight. He made *treaties* with nearby tribes and gathered a great army. Then Sundiata challenged the cruel king Sumanguru.

With lion-like courage, Sundiata won back his family's lands around the year 1235. Mali was set on a course to greatness with Sundiata leading the way.

Ghana declined late in the 1100s, and Sundiata began his reign in Mali about 1235. What was happening in the rest of the world at that time?

- Europe was a land of castles, farms, and bustling towns.

- In China, people were inventing gunpowder, the magnetic compass, and movable type for printing.

- In Central America, fierce Toltec Indians ruled the region now called Yucatan. They had just begun using stone pillars to support their roofs.

Think about these countries and others in the world during this time of prosperity in Africa. How do they compare with Mali?

Two Great Sultans of Mali

King Sundiata made Niani (nee-AH-nee), the city of his birth, his capital. The kingdom of Mali grew around this city located on the Niger River. From Niani, Sundiata started his own salt and gold trade. Then he led his armies westward and northward conquering lands. When new *borders* were established, Sundiata began ruling his empire.

Spread out over the grassy *plains* of West Africa, Mali had rich and fertile soil. At his suggestion, Sundiata's brave warriors became peaceful farmers. Before long Mali was producing some of the richest crops in the region. King Sundiata accomplished much in the twenty years he ruled Mali.

After Sundiata's death in 1255, Mali's new Muslim kings were called *Mansas* (MAHN-suhs) or *sultans*. Of all the kings to rule Mali, the greatest was Mansa Musa who took the throne early in the 1300s. His reign changed Mali forever.

Mansa Musa ruled Mali for twenty-five years. During that time he acquired huge areas of new land and extended Mali's borders widely. In spite of the empire's size, it had a fair, well-organized system of law and order. Mansa Musa continued the Muslim tradition of encouraging learning. He also supported art, literature, and architecture.

Learning is encouraged today as it was in Mansa Musa's time. What do you think these students in Mali are studying?

An Amazing Journey

In 1324 Mansa Musa made his required *hajj* (HAHJ), or holy trip to Mecca. Mecca is the holy city of the religion of Islam. It is located in what is now the nation of Saudi Arabia (SAH-dee uh-RAY-bee-uh). Followers of Islam believed then, as they do now, that making a hajj was their duty.

Thousands of followers from Mansa Musa's kingdom traveled with him on his hajj. He took along family members, friends, doctors, teachers, and local rulers.

His caravan was loaded down with food, supplies, and gold. There were one hundred camels, each bearing three hundred pounds of gold. Alongside the camels trudged five hundred slaves, each carrying a golden staff weighing four pounds. Mansa Musa traveled with huge amounts of gold to show the richness of his kingdom and to give *alms* (AHLMZ), or gifts to the needy. This was an important practice of his faith.

These children in Mali study the teachings of the *Koran*.

Along his journey, Mansa Musa visited with people in the parts of his empire through which he was passing. After leaving Mali he crossed the Sahara and made his way to Egypt.

When Mansa Musa reached the capital city of Cairo, Egypt, its *sultan* welcomed him warmly. In turn, a generous Mansa Musa gave gifts of gold to almost everyone he met. An Egyptian nobleman said the king "spread upon Cairo the flood of his generosity; there was no person . . . who did not receive a sum in gold from him." The people of Egypt long remembered the hajj of Mansa Musa. In fact, an Egyptian *historian* later declared it "the most outstanding event of 1324."

From Cairo, Mansa Musa continued to Mecca. Once there, he achieved his holy mission. He also achieved something else.

MORE ABOUT A HAJJ

A hajj is a religious trip to Mecca, the holy city of Islam. It was first undertaken to remind people of the Hejira (hih-JIH-ruh), Mohammad's journey to Mecca in the year 622. After that, the hajj became a requirement of the Muslim faith. Every devoted Muslim tries to make the journey at least once in a lifetime. It remains a Muslim duty today, even though the followers of Islam live all around the globe.

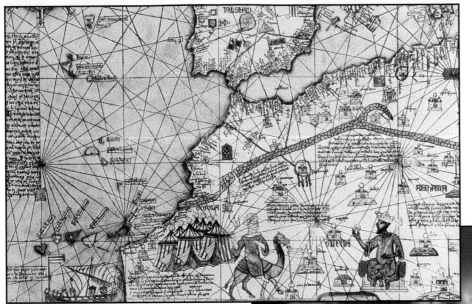

Mansa Musa became so well known throughout Europe because of his hajj that a map of Ghana with his picture on it was created.

His great show of wealth and power convinced many scholars, architects, and artists to return to Mali with him. Mansa Musa had a plan to make Mali a center for trade and education.

When they returned to Mali, one famous architect, Es-Saheli (ES-sah-HEHL-ee), built the University of Sankore in Timbuktu (tim-buk-TOO). This great university attracted students and teachers from all over the world. Mansa Musa encouraged learning by building many schools throughout his empire. He sent *ambassadors* to Egypt, Morocco, and all of North Africa to build friendly relations with their leaders. The love of learning spread throughout Mali.

A clay mosque in Timbuktu.

Splits Within the Empire

The name of Mansa Musa spread. From Egypt, stories of Mansa Musa's great hajj and the rich kingdom of Mali reached Europe. The civilizations of West Africa caught the interest of the rest of the world.

Mansa Musa died in 1337, leaving an empire so large that it was, in the words of one historian, "four months of travel long and four months wide." Upon his death, Mansa Musa's son, Maghan (MAHG-ahn), became king. Unfortunately, Maghan's *reign* was filled with problems. Invaders raided Timbuktu and set it on fire. Many years of progress in education were lost. Shortly after that, Mansa Maghan allowed two captured princes from neighboring Gao (GAH-oh) to escape. The new kingdom they founded would one day *conquer* Mali.

Mansa Maghan ruled for only four years. Then Sulayman (SOO-lay-mahn), Mansa Musa's brother, took the throne. Mansa Sulayman won back some of the lands lost under Maghan's reign and ruled Mali for eighteen years. After his death, the kingdom of Mali began to crumble. A series of weak rulers lost most of Mali's lands. By the 1400s, it was no longer a strong kingdom. All the while, the Songhai (Son-GAY) Empire in Gao was becoming stronger and stronger. ▓

TALK ABOUT IT

◎ The kings of Mali were heroes to their people. Who is your hero? Why do you admire that person?

◎ Mansa Musa used his great wealth to help his people. What would you do to help people today if you were a rich king?

◎ Why do you think Mansa Musa thought learning was important for his people? Do you think learning is more important or less important today than it was then? Why?

WRITE ABOUT IT

Suppose you were the king or queen of Mali, an empire made up of many kinds of people with different customs and languages. How would you rule them? What would you do to be sure each area was fairly treated? Write a plan that you might use to govern your empire.

3

The next great empire of ancient West Africa— Songhai—rose to power during the late 1400s. This empire would become more advanced and grow larger in area and population than either Ghana or Mali.

THE EMPIRE OF SONGHAI

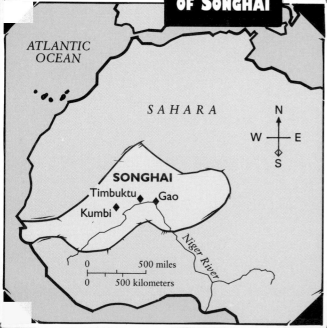

ATLANTIC OCEAN

SAHARA

N
W · E
S

SONGHAI

Timbuktu ◆ ◆ Gao

Kumbi ◆

Niger River

0   500 miles
0   500 kilometers

Sultan Sunni Ali of ancient Gao escaping from Mali.

THE TRIUMPH OF SONGHAI

The empire of Songhai was governed by the noble Sultan Sunni Ali (SOO-nee AH-lee) in the year 1464. Ruling from the city of Gao, he saw the strength of neighboring Mali fade and the strength of his own kingdom, Songhai, increase. Strangely, he had been a captive in Mali only a few years before. Now he was building an empire that would overpower that kingdom.

Sunni Ali was more than just a noble king. He was a great warrior who at first ruled Songhai from the battlefield. The empire expanded under the leadership of this fierce ruler. Sunni Ali spent so much time fighting in different parts of Songhai, he kept four palaces in operation at once.

One by one he defeated other tribes who raided his lands. Then he looked to the west—to Mali—and conquered the great cities Jenne (juh-NAY) and Timbuktu. He appointed governors to care for each of the *provinces* of the empire. He kept a navy that patrolled the Niger River. He set up a huge army equipped with armor, horses and camels.

Then in 1492, at the height of his power, Sunni Ali's rule ended in a very unexpected way. Legends tell that while crossing a swift stream he was swept off his horse and was drowned. The death of Sunni Ali paved the way for perhaps the greatest Songhai ruler of all, Askia Muhammad (AHS-kee-uh moo-HAM-uhd), to gain power.

Askia the Great

Shortly after Sunni Ali's death, one of his top commanders, Askia Muhammad, seized the throne of Songhai. Askia overthrew Sunni Ali's son who had ruled for a short time.

Under Sultan Askia, the Songhai Empire reached the peak of its glory and African culture flowered as never before. He welcomed teachers, doctors, poets, students, religious leaders, and lawyers to Songhai.

Concerned about education, Askia built schools in Gao, Timbuktu, and Jenne. These schools drew educated people from as far away as Europe and Asia. Students from many nations studied alongside Songhai students. They learned grammar, law, literature, art,

Top: Bronze sculpture of a king created by a skilled West African artist.

Bottom: The outside of the tomb of Askia the Great of Songhai who died in 1538. What do you think should be written on the walls about this great king?

government, mathematics, geography, and medicine, as well as music and poetry. Askia himself studied religion.

Because he was a strong believer in Islam, Askia decided to make a hajj in 1495. With him went five hundred mounted soldiers and one thousand soldiers on foot. As Mansa Musa had done over a century before, Askia brought along a huge amount of gold. He planned to give alms to the needy and buy expensive gifts.

Askia's holy journey took two years. When he returned to Songhai he found his empire in good order. This made him anxious to fight *jihads* (jee-HAHDS), or holy wars, to conquer more lands for the religion of Islam.

Askia's jihads made Songhai one of the largest empires in Africa at this time. The sultan expanded his lands far beyond what earlier kings had dreamed possible. He conquered smaller kingdoms and took captives.

Once he had established his empire's borders, Askia Muhammad turned his attention to keeping his lands in order. He improved the system of government. He divided Songhai into five sections, each headed by a governor who reported directly to him. He kept an army and a navy, and set up a system of banks. Now that Songhai was at peace, trade increased and merchants from Europe and Asia became regular visitors.

CURRENCY IN THE SONGHAI EMPIRE

As trading grew in ancient Africa, so did the need for some form of currency or money. Paper money and coins, such as the modern world uses, did not yet exist there. Until the mid-fifteenth century, cowrie shells and "trading beads" were used as currency. Among some West African peoples, iron chains and spearheads were also considered forms of money. Then, in the mid-1400s, while the Songhai Empire was rising, coins became popular. Of course then, as now, nuggets of gold had great value and were also used to buy goods.

Timbuktu, Center of Learning

Although Gao was the city from which Sultan Askia ruled, Timbuktu became the empire's main center of learning. Its universities became known all over the world.

Visitors to that city found it a huge, interesting home to more than 100,000 people. Two great mosques of stone and lime stood taller than any other city buildings. They were surrounded by flat-roofed, wood-and-plaster houses of the citizens. Facing the narrow streets were factories and shops where visitors could buy almost anything they could need. In the markets, foods like grains, fruits, milk, and butter could be bought. Cotton cloth, gold and silver jewelry, and other goods were also for sale. Many merchants came to Timbuktu in huge numbers from as far away as Europe. They had goods to sell and African goods they wanted to buy.

Top: The wealthy city of Timbuktu as it appeared to an early traveler.
Below: Local market scene in modern day Timbuktu. How is this scene similar to ancient Timbuktu?

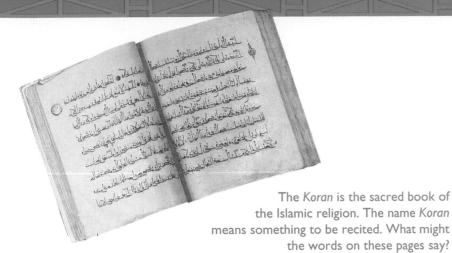

The *Koran* is the sacred book of the Islamic religion. The name *Koran* means something to be recited. What might the words on these pages say?

Scholars from the great universities mingled there with rich merchants. Students sat in the shade studying the **Koran,** the holy book of Islam. In addition to the temples, schools, shops, and factories, were libraries and bookstores. An historian wrote, "There is a big demand for books in manuscript, imported from Barbary [North Africa]. More profit is made from the book trade than from any other line of business."

Timbuktu was also known to have excellent hospitals where advanced medicine was practiced with much success. Doctors there used the newest methods for treating all illnesses. One historian recorded that in Timbuktu his brother underwent a delicate eye operation and later went home completely cured.

Compare this person baking in Timbuktu to how you prepare food at home.

The late 1400s was an exciting time. All over the world people were developing new ideas and discovering new things. You will probably think first of Christopher Columbus. He landed in the Bahama Islands in 1492. What else was happening at this time?

- **Copernicus**, the Polish founder of modern astronomy, had come up with an astounding new theory. He believed Earth was a moving planet.

- **The Incas** of South America had mastered complicated architecture, sculpture, weaving, and pottery making.

- **Leonardo Da Vinci**, Italian painter and sculptor, sketched images of what would become the first airplanes.

- **The Hopi Indian** people of North America were using coal in complex heating systems.

- **Martin Benhaim**, a German, had built the first known globe of the world.

Which of these do you think has most affected your life today?

A modern West African celebration.

The people of Timbuktu loved socializing and welcomed occasions to have celebrations. Both men and women would dress in rich clothing and wear a great deal of gold and jewelry. Often the music and dancing went on far into the night. The Songhai people also enjoyed fencing, poetry readings, gymnastics, and games such as chess.

This is what one famous historian had to say about Timbuktu when he visited the city in 1526:

> Here are many shops of artificers [craftspeople] and merchants . . . the Barbary merchants bring cloth of Europe. All the women of this region, except the maid-servants, go with their faces covered, and sell all necessary victuals [food]. The inhabitants . . . are exceeding rich, insomuch that the king . . . married both his daughters to rich merchants. Here are many wells containing most sweet water . . .

The Invasion of West Africa

At the same time Songhai was advancing, traders from Portugal and later other European nations had reached the shores of West Africa. They wanted its riches for themselves.

Traders had already set up trading bases along the Atlantic coast when they heard an important rumor. The sultan of Morocco, a kingdom located in northwest Africa, wanted to invade Songhai. The Europeans decided to help him, hoping he in turn would open more trade. So they gave the sultan something never before seen in Africa—*harquebuses* (HAHR-kwuh-buhsez), or guns, to arm all of his soldiers.

In 1590, after nine years of planning, the sultan of Morocco sent an army across the Sahara toward Songhai. The four thousand men were led by a Spanish Muslim named Judar Pasha. It took Judar five months to reach Gao which was now ruled by Askia Ishag II. After marching through sandstorms with hardly any water, only a thousand of Judar's soldiers were left. Gao was defended by nearly 30,000 soldiers on foot and on horseback armed with bows and arrows, and spears.

Africans used hand weapons like this one to fight their battles.

The French soldier here is holding a harquebus, which is the kind of gun Moroccans used when attacking Songhai.

The weapons made all the difference in the battle. Against guns, even the best spears, bows, or arrows were useless. The soldiers of Songhai were frightened by the noise and smoke of the guns. They were confused by the strange deaths of their fellow soldiers. Unstopped, Judar Pasha marched through Songhai taking great riches wherever he found them.

The invaded empire of Songhai became weak. Its army defeated, it was left unprotected. The empire's trade vanished, cities declined, and the central government collapsed. Without peace and safety, the wealth of Songhai disappeared. The sultan of Morocco had won the land, but lost the kingdom's riches. ◆

TALK ABOUT IT

◎ The students of Songhai studied many subjects. Which of these are the same subjects you study? If you were setting up your own school, what would you have the students learn about?

◎ Think about the description of the city of Timbuktu. Of what present-day cities does it remind you? Why?

◎ Askia Muhammad took 300,000 pieces of gold with him on his hajj. If you were traveling on a hajj, what things would you take along? What would you use for money?

WRITE ABOUT IT

Historians have written about what the people of Songhai liked to do for enjoyment. What can you learn about these people from this information? What would people of the future learn about us if they read about modern games, sports, and hobbies? Write a brief description of modern American pastimes to be included in a time capsule which will be opened and read by someone in the year 2500.

4

When the Songhai Empire was conquered, the glory of West Africa declined too. All that was left was a handful of tiny kingdoms fighting each other. Their fighting and need for money and weapons made them eager to trade with Europeans. Africa's people would become a most prized resource. ◆◆

Captured Africans were taken from the coast of Africa in small boats to board large trading ships.

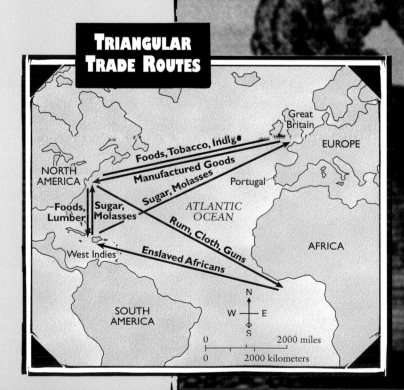

TRIANGULAR TRADE ROUTES

Great Britain

EUROPE

NORTH AMERICA

Foods, Tobacco, Indigo

Manufactured Goods

Sugar, Molasses

Portugal

ATLANTIC OCEAN

Foods, Lumber

Sugar, Molasses

Rum, Cloth, Guns

AFRICA

West Indies

Enslaved Africans

SOUTH AMERICA

N
W   E
S

0   2000 miles
0   2000 kilometers

THE SLAVE TRADE

Slave ships filled with Africans followed a shipping pattern known as the *triangular trade*. On the first part of the triangle, European ships sailed to West Africa carrying cheap goods and guns. These goods were traded for African captives. On the next leg of the trip, the captives were brought to the Americas and sold to *plantation* owners for sugar, rum, raw cotton, and tobacco. On the last leg of the triangle, these goods were then taken back across the Atlantic Ocean to Europe. Often traders made profits five times greater than their expenses.

Some Africans were traded as part of peaceful bargains. Other Africans were kidnapped and forced into slavery. A young African boy described his and his sister's kidnapping with these words:

> One day, when all our people were gone out to their work as usual, and only I and my sister were left to mind the house, two men and a woman got over our walls, and in a moment seized us both; and without giving us time to cry out, or to make any resistance, they stopped our mouths and ran off with us into the nearest woods. Here they tied our hands, and continued to carry us as far as they could...

The boy, Olaudah Equiano (OH-lah-dah e-QUEE-ah-noh), was kidnapped at a time when the Europeans had been trading for African slaves for over two hundred years. He was only eleven years old when captured. He was the son of an African chief of the Ibo (EE-boh) people and had lived in Benin, West Africa, surrounded by a loving family. But that day in 1756 changed his life forever.

For two days after Equiano's capture the African kidnappers trudged through the forest. They carried Equiano and his sister bound and gagged in sacks. Then on the fourth morning, Equiano and his sister were separated. Years later he recorded his feelings about the separation.

It was in vain that we besought [begged] them not to part us, but she was torn from me, and immediately carried away, while I was left in a state of distraction not to be described. I cried and grieved continually; and for several days did not eat anything but what they forced into my mouth.

Journey to the Atlantic

By 1870, between ten and twelve million Africans had been captured and sent to the Americas. Most historians agree that the first African kings who sold other Africans to the Europeans did not realize to what this would lead. After all, slavery had long been practiced among them. Trading people to Europeans seemed natural.

African kings first traded captives they had taken in wars. They also traded their own people who had broken laws. Women and children were traded less often. Later many of those who became enslaved were forcefully kidnapped by European traders. After thousands of people had been sold into *bondage*, some African kings protested. By then no one was listening.

Like the great West African kings in ancient times, this local Ashanti chief in modern Ghana is directly responsible to his people. The umbrella symbolizes the chief's authority.

The slave trade of Africans to countries outside of Europe grew slowly. Sugar and cotton plantations of North and South America needed workers. Owners of these plantations had first enslaved Indians. The Indians quickly began to die from the hard physical work and European sicknesses. The Spanish then looked across the oceans to West Africa for laborers. Equiano was to become one of these enslaved workers.

Many Africans shared the same experiences that Equiano had. After his capture, Equiano eventually began his journey on foot to the ocean. He was yoked to

other captives by logs and chains. In addition to Equiano's people, the Mandingos, the Yorubas (yoh-RUH-baz), the Benis (BIN-is), and other African peoples were among those taken as captives. Those who fought back or were too weak to keep up, were speared and left on the trail. On this long and difficult march, two out of every five captives died.

Upon reaching the coast of the Atlantic Ocean, the captured Africans were herded into warehouses called *barracoons* (bahr-ah-KOONS). These warehouses were part of huge forts slave traders had built. There European traders representing many companies chose the captives they wanted. They offered cloth, knives, guns, rum, gunpowder, and glass beads to Africans for the captives. As deals were made, each captive was branded with a red-hot iron to show who the owner was. Then groups were chained together again and marched down to the beach.

Europeans built "slave factories" or trading forts like this one along the coast of West Africa.

One-Way Passage to America

Many of the Africans were terrified. Some threw themselves onto the beach, helplessly clawing at the sand. Others tried to strangle themselves with their chains.

Aboard a British ship, Equiano and the other men were forced into the hold, or cargo area. Their ankles were clamped with leg irons and they were forced to lie close together. Other captives lay on shelves above them, and still others lay in small spaces between the rows. They were packed so tightly that none of them could even sit up.

With some four hundred Africans crowded together, the air soon became so foul that many grew sick and died. Some captives went mad from grief and fear. Women, especially those with children, usually were not chained. However, they suffered as the men did, fearing most that their children would be harmed.

Every morning and afternoon the captives were taken onto the deck to be fed. Their leg irons were fastened to a great chain that ran the length of the ship. They were usually given a meal of boiled rice, corn meal, or stewed yams, and a half-pint of water. Afterward, under the threat of sailors with whips, the Africans were forced to dance or jump around. This

Top: Hand and leg irons like these were used to keep African captives from escaping.
Bottom: Africans in this cargo hold were "loosely" packed because they were able to lie flat. Africans who were "tightly" packed lay on their sides.

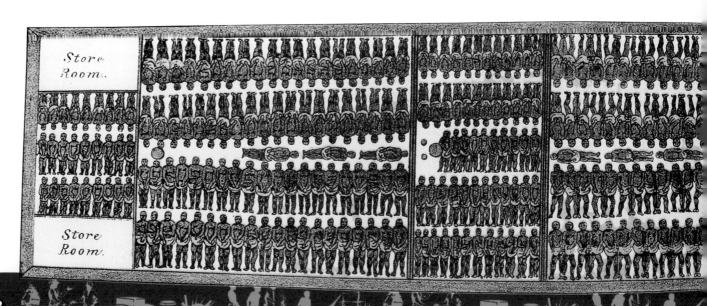

routine of "dancing the slaves" was done to be sure the captives stayed in as good physical shape as possible. Otherwise buyers in the Americas might not want them.

The Africans tried bravely to resist captivity at every opportunity. Some refused to eat, choosing starvation over a life of slavery. But the traders often whipped them cruelly until they ate. Sometimes an iron bar was used to force their mouths open. At other times, the captives' teeth were broken and food was poured down their throats.

Africans who became sick were thrown overboard to keep disease from spreading. Measles, smallpox, scurvy, and other illnesses claimed many lives. So high was the rate of death that "loss of cargo" ranged from a few captives to as many as half of the shipment.

Equiano described his feelings aboard ship. "The shrieks of the women, and the groans of the dying, rendered it a scene of horror . . . I expected every hour to share the fate of my companions, some of whom were almost daily brought up on deck at the point of death, and I began to hope that death would soon put an end to my miseries."

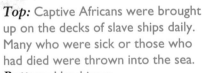

Top: Captive Africans were brought up on the decks of slave ships daily. Many who were sick or those who had died were thrown into the sea. *Bottom:* Hand irons.

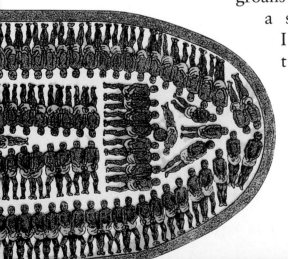

Top: People came from everywhere to bid on Africans at slave auctions.
Bottom: Posters like this one announced the arrival of Africans to be sold as slaves.

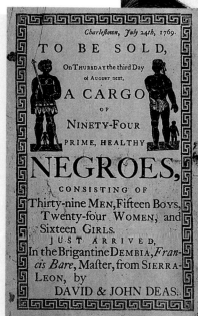

Charlestown, July 24th, 1769.

TO BE SOLD,

On THURSDAY the third Day of AUGUST next,

A CARGO

OF

NINETY-FOUR

PRIME, HEALTHY

NEGROES,

CONSISTING OF

Thirty-nine MEN, Fifteen BOYS, Twenty-four WOMEN, and Sixteen GIRLS.

JUST ARRIVED,

In the Brigantine DEMBIA, *Francis Bare*, Master, from SIERRA-LEON, by

DAVID & JOHN DEAS.

An Unknown Land

After several weeks at sea, the slave ship docked at one of the islands of the West Indies. There Equiano and the other Africans were sold as slave laborers. Equiano described the slave merchants who met the ship:

At last we came in sight of the island of Barbados, at which the whites on board gave a great shout . . . . We did not know what to think of this, but . . . we plainly saw the harbour, and other ships of different kinds and sizes . . . . Many merchants and planters now came on board . . . . They put us in separate parcels, and examined us attentively. They also made us jump, and pointed to the land, signifying we were to go there. We thought by this we should be beaten by these ugly men . . . and . . . there was much dread and trembling among us.

After their sale, the enslaved Africans were taught discipline and how to do whatever work was needed. They might serve in houses, in mines, or in the sugar cane fields. This training process, called seasoning, often broke the bodies as well as the spirits of the captives. As many as one third of the Africans died from overwork, sickness, and the whip during the seasoning process.

The Africans who survived seasoning soon learned ways to cope with their hardships. Whenever possible, they spoke their native language and practiced the customs of their homelands. Although given "slave" names, they often used their birth names among themselves. They did not willingly forget from where they had come.

SEASONING IN THE WEST INDIES

The "seasoning" of Africans usually lasted from three to four years. This process often took place in the West Indies on sugar plantations. By the mid-1600s, the demand for sugar was so high that European ships carried up to ten thousand enslaved Africans a year to the West Indies to work. There were also cotton, spice, and dyewood plantations on these islands.

Africans who would eventually go to the American colonies were often taken to the West Indies to go through "seasoning."

Each African was given a work assignment of repeating a task for twelve hours each day. This way they could be introduced to the realities of slave life, and broken into the proper behaviors expected of enslaved persons in America.

The West Indian economy was based on African slave labor.

TALK ABOUT IT

◎ Equiano wrote about many of his terrible experiences. If you could speak to Equiano today, what questions would you ask him?

◎ By 1870, over ten million Africans had been sold into slavery. What effect do you think the departure of those millions of people had on the continent of Africa?

◎ Why do you think the trading of Africans as slaves began? Why didn't the people who bought enslaved Africans simply have other people work for them?

WRITE ABOUT IT

You are an educated person living during the time of the triangular trade. You are horrified by slavery and do all you can to fight it. Write an article for your local newspaper persuading your readers that slavery must not be allowed to continue.

ECHOES
OF EARLY AFRICA

The voices of the people of ancient Africa tell us stories of highly developed civilizations that existed there. The accounts of the educated people and strong leaders of West Africa add details of wealthy kingdoms and fascinating cultures. What in these stories tells you why these people prospered as they did? Why do you think their civilizations later declined?

The West African kingdoms had developed excellent ways to trade, educate, and protect themselves. What can we learn from these civilizations? What more would you like to learn about these people?

The ancient African civilizations were highly developed long before those of some European and Asian neighbors. What effect do you think the Africans' accomplishments have had on the modern world? How might our world be different if African people had never existed?

3200 BC
The Egyptian civilization begins.

400 BC
Rise of the Kingdom of Axum.

1236
Sundiata becomes King of Mali.

1235
The Kingdom of Mali grows and develops.

1324
Mansa Musa makes his hajj to Mecca.

1337
Mansa Musa's son, Maghan, rules Mali.

⦿ 4000 ⦿ 3000 ⦿ 2000 ⦿ 1000 ⦿ 0 1300 ⦿

750 BC
Kingdom of Kush is established.

1065
Tunka Manin rules Ghana.

1312
Mansa Musa rules Mali.

1100
Ghana begins to decline in power.

1341
Mansa Sulayman becomes ruler of Mali.

1400
The Kingdom of Songhai begins to rise to power.

1464
Sultan Sunni Ali rules Songhai.

1492
Askia Muhammad seizes the Songhai throne.

1619
Captured Africans are brought to the colony of Jamestown.

1513
The trans-Atlantic slave trade begins.

1800
Millions of Africans being captured and sent to the Americas.

⊙ **1400** ⊙ **1500** ⊙ **1600** ⊙ **1700** **1800** ⊙

1441
Prince Henry of Portugal sends explorers to the west coast of Africa.

1502
The first African laborers arrive in the West Indies.

1756
Olaudah Equiano is kidnapped from West Africa.

1460
About 600 Africans are enslaved in Portugal every year.

1590
Morocco conquers Songhai.

1482
Portuguese slave traders build fort in West Africa.

GLOSSARY

alms • *(AHLMZ)* • Items such as money, gifts, and food, given to help poor people.

ambassador • *(am BAS uh dor)* • The highest representative of a government working and living in another country.

barracoon • *(bar u KOON)* • An enclosure used to temporarily confine slaves awaiting transportation.

barter • *(BAHR tuhr)* • The trading of goods for other goods or services.

border • *(BOR dur)* • The location where two places touch or meet.

captive • (KAP tiv) • A person caught and held prisoner, as in war.

caravan • *(CAR uh van)* • A group of people traveling together for safety, especially through a desert.

conquer • *(KAHN kir)* • To get or gain by using force, as by winning a war.

desert • *(DEZ urt)* • A very dry place, with little rainfall and few plants.

empire • *(IM peyer)* • A group of countries or territories under the control of one ruler.

enslaved • *(in SLAYVD)* • To be made to work for no wages or pay.

grasslands • *(GRAS lands)* • Lands with grass growing on them.

hajj • *(HAHJ)* • A pilgrimage to the holy city of Mecca that most Muslims try to make at least once.

harquebus • *(HAHR kwuh buhs)* • An early type of portable gun.

historian • *(his TOHR ee an)* • A writer of histories or an expert who writes the details of time and place.

Islam • *(IS lom)* • The Muslim religion, founded by Mohammed, in which God is called Allah.

jihad • *(jee HAHD)* • A Muslim war against unbelievers or enemies of Islam, carried out as a religious duty.

GLOSSARY

Koran • *(koh RAN)* • The sacred book of Islam.

Mansa • *(MANS ah)* • A title given to Muslim kings in ancient Africa.

merchant • *(MUR chunt)* • A person who buys and sells goods.

mineral • *(MIN ur uhl)* • A substance obtained by mining or digging in the earth.

mosque • *(MOSK)* • Muslim place of worship.

Muslim • *(MOOZ lim)* • A believer in the religion of Islam.

plains • *(PLAYNS)* • Wide, open areas of flat or rolling lands.

plantation • *(plan TAY shun)* • A large farm which mainly grows one crop.

province • *(PROV ins)* • A region in or belonging to a country, having its own local governments.

reign • *(RAYN)* • To rule or the length of the rule of a king or queen.

silent trade • *(SEYE lint TRAYD)* • A form of trading in which no words are spoken.

sultan • *(SUL tun)* • A ruler of Muslim countries, especially in earlier times.

tax • *(TAKS)* • Money that must be paid to a government.

throne • *(THROHN)* • The raised chair on which a king sits during ceremonies.

treaties • *(TREET ees)* • Formal agreements, either spoken or written.

triangular trade • *(treye ANG yoo lur TRAYD)* • Trade routes toward and away from the American colonies that formed a triangle.

Index 〜〜〜〜〜〜〜〜〜〜〜〜〜〜〜〜〜〜〜〜